Ghost Dogs

Ghost Dogs

Dion O'Reilly

Terrapin Books

Terrapin Books
4 Midvale Avenue
West Caldwell, NJ 07006

www.terrapinbooks.com

ISBN: 978-1-947896-23-9
LCCN: 2019953521

First Edition

Cover art: *Running Coyotes*
Mixed Media on Tyvek 60"x 120"
by Myra Eastman

For Arthur and Darrian because twins were my destiny,
and for Michael, my best surprise

In loving memory of my river sister Suzie

Contents

Insides

On cold mornings, as he stropped his blade
on the wand of the whetstone,
the butcher would tell me how he loved
warming his hands inside a steaming beast,
and I, a child, held out for him
the steel bucket for the bull's heart,
big as a rugby ball, still beating,
its convent of small passages, matrixed
with muscle and stiff fat. I carried it,
with the vast plain of liver,
the kidneys and pimply tongue—
three trips at least—through the wet
vetch and bees, bringing every bit
of this bounty to my mother
to fry in butter—quick—
before the raw power waned.

Ode to High Tea

Apricot pie, lemon bars, scones, water biscuits
bland as hardtack, laid out by Mother
on three-tiered cake stands.
Barely tall enough, I put water to boil,
the kettle, a blustering blowhard with a whistle.
Fat belly of the pot heated and dried,
teaspoons of fine-cut tea inside:
Assam, Keemun, and Ceylon
re-mixed every season, despite droughts
or blight, typhoons, heat, crop failure,
every cup the same harsh flush, year after year.

Quick, pull the cozy over the pot, keep it hot
no matter the endless California sun, how far
from cold emerald fields.
Which of the bone china: roses, willow, forget-me-not?
Wait three minutes, steep it strong, dark as forest mud,
add milk, stir to creamy brown. The steam
smells of barn grain, winter bogs, dried alfalfa.
The sugar habit gone from rationing in the war,
but the bowl of white cubes with sterling pinchers
stands on the table for symmetry with the pitcher.
Folded napkins, little beds for the spoons,
forks sharp at the ready.
Mother checks I set the table straight,
her wet flannel dishcloth snaps
like a whip on the back of my head,
rubs rough across my face.
Through my matted hair, she yanks
a fine-tooth comb.

Grandmother crosses the bridge,
then through the gate in her red lipstick, shooing
the drooling mastiffs from her yellow dress.
My sister with her current boy.
Maybe my father leaves his den
to join us for a while in the kitchen.

We don't know if Typhoo brand
is hand-picked or pan-fried,
if it's carried on the heads of porters
a hundred miles across mud valleys, through
the freezing passes of Two Wolves Mountain.

For the time it takes the afternoon light to cross the room,
we lift cups to our lips, taste how sun and mountain
mists cured the leaves from thousand-year-old trees.

Mare in the Road

Midnight, the blacktop in front of me
familiar in the headlights and coastal fog.
Suddenly, horses, shiny with sweaty coats,
careen across my path, racketing
like an avalanche, twenty or so, in an instant
before they gallop down a ravine.

Gone, except one, still standing
on three good legs. Struck
by a car speeding around the bend
or kicked in the bucking frenzy,
stranded now, immobile.
I pull over, walk to the chestnut mare,
her head down, ears quivering and veined
like sable leaves, her smell strong
like sap from an old tree.

She looks at me—her eyes
a full glazed brown—
then moves her head violently,
like nodding *Yes*.
No halter, so I pull at the forelock
and click softly, nudging her away
from the danger. It's so hard
with her cannon bone,
the long one below the knee, bent
like a broken branch.
But she blows out her wet nostrils,
limps off the bloody road
to the shoulder where we wait.

When the vet finally arrives,
I stand, one hand on the blaze
crowning her forehead, the other squeezing
the muscled crest of her neck,
and her life—

the onion smell of meadows, the small
warm herds, the shimmering leaves in the wind—
all of it canters away in the darkness.

Scars

From playing barefoot all summer,
running up trees, the bud of a new branch
piercing me. Stitchery buried
now under the hoofy remains
of a burn that swept up
my legs like a prairie blaze

when a spark from the fireplace torched me,
branded my fleeing tracks in the rug.
Doctors tilled the earth of my foot
grafted a net of skin there, the older,
spidery line gone, one pain
subsumed by another,

like knee-bruises of childhood,
a twice-broken elbow, lost
to the young man whose eyes at night
were a constellation I knew by heart,
who softened me
into saying yes, and then forgot me.

And years later, carrying twins—
toxemia, edema, my failing heart and kidneys—
all that trouble, obscured
by the grip of childbirth,
the improbable distortion
when the first head split through,
and that erased, twelve minutes later
by the next. All forgotten
in the stinging sleeplessness, the hours
blending in a long dirging love song
of crying, colic, plugged breasts.

When I study my layers of proud flesh
and the long history of the world, I wonder
if there are lacerations so deep
there is no greater pain.
But there's always something worse.
A girl slices her arm, wanting the slash
to dull another torment: she knows
who raped her. The next wound
would be to speak his name.

Why Did I Call My Pig?

I watched my mother call her,
watched my sister too.
My father tried to catch her.
She was quick, my piebald oinker.
Her squeals greased the air.

She knew the jig was up,
ran to the farthest corner, down
by the creek and the steep ravine,
hid in shadows under oak trees,
rooting prickled leaves and acorns
with her wet ringed snout.

My huge baby, companion
on aimless teenage days
when I balanced on the fencepost,
listening to her belly-deep rumble,
stick-scratched her itchy,
thick-skinned back.

The butcher with a rifle,
stood impatient by his Chevy truck,
its hook and chain ready
to haul the limp sow up,
to scrape the skin and slice the stomach
in a thin red line, bowels spilling
glazy as moonstones.

Forgive me. To show off my small power,
I called her—the one she loved—
and she came running.

Liberal Father

He sits in thinned Hanes, reading
The New Republic, one leg crossed over the other—
picking at a flaked green toenail,
some rot caught in the steaming air
during amphibious assault on Guadalcanal.

On weekends under wraiths of blue smoke,
he visits with his buddies—
men in striped bell-bottoms and Afros,
women with long noses and gypsy earrings,
French professors from the university—
organizing for the first farmworker for Congress,
the first Black man for president, the next Kennedy.

At five, he rises like a machine, feeds the mastiffs,
leaves to teach high school, his Civics students
invading the City Council, printing T-shirts in the garage,
storming a precinct in Watsonville, registering voters
around the vinegar plant, the lined-up shanties
by the cabbage field.

He fortifies the teachers' union with longshoremen,
brings in the NAACP to meet the environmentalists.
You gotta get 'em talking, he tells me.
Like Tip and the Gipper. Everyone lifted up.

Except my sister and me, when—
together with my mother—he sets upon us
with whip and belt. Their cheeks, as they beat us,
red as bruises, eyes glazed
like they're having sex.
Until I turn nine, his fist suspended over me,

I stand in front of the dead fireplace,
a piece of sharp kindling in my hand,
prepared to kill them both.

Doreen, he says, *I'm not doing this shit anymore.*
So she beats us herself
while he stays out till midnight
attending meetings at the League of Women Voters.

Pilgrim

They don't look where they're going
as they drive their mud-caked trucks and Subarus
along the crumbled cliffs at Pleasure Point—

the surfers, twisting their spines for a glimpse of Sewer Peak
or gazing at an angle toward The Hook, seeking the swells
that curl around the reefs, the high wedges that crunch the shore.

They can't stop travelling west, an endless summer
of shore breaks and peak breaks to a sun that never sets.

I knew a man who wanted me like that.

He followed me like a pilgrim in pursuit of a saint,
his truck an immaculate chapel, offerings stowed
in the glove box or swinging from the rear-view.

When we met, he laid his gifts before me on his palm—
tithes of rhinestones, strands of faux sapphires,
dolls with waxy faces, sunglasses of green celluloid.

So I let him have me.

And after, his face scoured clean, radiant like a child's,
he confessed his sins—the daughters he'd abandoned,
his angry wives—said he knew I could save him.

But soon he tired of me, no longer cruising by my driveway
as I left in the morning, no cards lush with Rossetti paintings
in my mailbox, no deep-blue feathers torn

from a dead jay's wing, tucked in an envelope.
He died years ago, but I still think of him

when I see those smooth barefoot bodies with nothing
but towels knotted at their waists as they pull
neoprene skins up their legs and cold-nippled torsos,
then run away toward the pumping waves.

I can't help hoping I'll see him, still searching for me
in his Studebaker pickup and ruined straw hat.

Scavenged

*... what becomes
of us once we've been torn apart
and returned to our future ...*
—Dorianne Laux

When I was nineteen, a flame clung to my back,
ate me to the spine. Torch-lit and alone,
I ran through the house, a contagion
cindering couches and carpets.
Flayed, my fingertips peeled back
to the nail beds. My spongy tissues touched air,
light, and the steel cot where they took me.

Each day, they peeled me
like Velcro from my sheets,
left bits of my meat there.
Lowered me into Betadine,
scrubbed me to screams—
that became my history. Scavenged
by the curious. They see my twisted fingers
and are hungry for the tale.

I've done the same, stared
at a leg's nubbed end, wanted to touch it,
feel the cut bone under the knob,
hear its shrapnel story. I wanted to know
how that man was alive, arms glistening
playing basketball from a high-tech chair,
making his shots.

The body's scarred terrain becomes
consecrated field. We gather to pick
through the pieces that remain—

an ear hanging from its hinge of skin,
diamond stud in the lobe, ring finger
shining with its promise-band of gold.

Dead Dog

When I find her behind the barn,
she's feeding pellets to the Rhode Island Reds,
the Plymouth Rocks, and Buff Orpington hens,
the strutting cockerel she plans to cook.

My mother looks up when she hears me,
and I wonder if she's sick. So baby-like
around the eyes and the pinch of her mouth.
A heavy feed bucket pulls her to one side
as she limps toward me, opens her lips

so wide, I'm afraid she'll vomit.
Instead, she tells me she killed her father's dog
sixty-five years ago. It was my grandmother
who made her do it—a jealous woman
who wanted her husband to love only her.
Now my mother, nearly ninety, weeps
as she confesses: *He never stopped looking for that dog.*

I listen and wonder at her choice
of regret. Why not the hot, wet washcloths
slapped across my face at dinner?
The purple slash of the bullwhip?
The way she slung my small body
onto the backs of unbroke horses,
let the ground bend my bones?

I feel a weakness in my thighs
like I'm catching the flu, her suffering
ambushes my white blood cells,
roughs up the tissues of my throat.
I almost feel sorry for her, until
I look down at my miraculous body.
Lucky. Alive.

II

Given

If my family were never allowed an American morning
of low-interest home loans given to White boys
like my dad—returned from the war demented
by jungle juice, the ear-sting of mortar fire,
but ready for Stanford on the veteran dole.

And if he never bought *World Book Encyclopedias,*
left them around for me to look at any time I wanted,
with all those endless facts about planets and Max Planck,
or the hardbacks he gave me about pioneers in a dug-out
protected by a bulldog and a shotgun—
without that, would I have known what I wanted
was of the mind and its nimble mirrors?

Look what I had— a ranch, the land empty, a wide wilderness
of neglect stretching between the daily harms
of my mother with her Elizabeth Taylor eyes
and home-butchered rabbit stole.
She lent me the hours when she threw me away—
all the time I wanted to inspect wolf spiders and wade
in river shallows, to hide behind a wet bar
and suck my thumb, rub the blanket's
silk edge on my cheek, hold a book
close to my face like a beloved.

Is there a way to make it wonderful?
Bone bruises purpling the points of my patella,
knees dragged over gravel and ground-in with mud,
my mom red-hot with disgust when I couldn't
chase chickens into cages.

I would go downtown to Woolworth's, find
DC comics spinning on a wire altar, read

about a girl in a red cape, see words
like *orphan baby from a blown-up world saves the Earth.*
Buy them for an easy dime and two pennies,
found glittering casually on the closet floor
among the many colors of my mother's high-heeled shoes.

Rivervale

We slammed screen doors. We set out shoeless
on paths of powdery sand, smelled
the pockets of cool air rank with black mud.
Maple trees leaned in and dropped leaves
that rested like bruised hands on the skin of the water.

None of our mother's bitched-out tasks.
No pimped-out sisters or fatherless boys.
No patch-eyed stepfathers drunk in La-Z-Boys.
Gone the stench of spilled beer and rat turds.
We learned *downstream*. We learned *leaving*. We learned *someday*.

Herons lifted their great bodies from the streambed,
shining fish caught in their tapered beaks,
and the agony twisting in the air made sense.
We looked to the world beneath the clear surface
with its teeming minnows. We pushed shin-deep
through the creek, crawdads hiding, black pincers pointing out.
We snatched steelhead and trout. We drank the water.

Afterlife

In the hot summers of childhood,
we waded a mile in the river—
you, up against the current,
and I, down toward the sea.
And we screamed like bloody birds,
so before we met at the bend,
I heard your calls strafe the air.

And then we stood, face to face,
at a fattening of the river,
next to a beach, rough with granite and quartz,
minnows' lips on our legs,
a cold ache in our feet,
shadows of water skeeters—
like bunches of black grapes—
flickering along the floor.

Suzie, I never lost you
through the brutal climb
of our twenties, our failed marriages,
your treks to Kauai, your plummets
down the ski runs of Bear Valley.
When we'd meet, you'd kiss me on the lips,
tell me Schnapps cured a cold,
say you liked waking up higher,
close to the sun,
so you settled in gold country,
waiting tables and selling real estate—
then, at fifty-four, you were gone,
your stomach full of bourbon and Oxycontin.

I still live on the same stream-cut terrace
high above the dwindling creek.
Your mom's old house on the floodplain—
sold—full of strangers.
I wish I could tell you how seldom
I go to the bottomland, how there are gates
on the trails, and the land, disgruntled,
sends up walls of slick poison oak.
How the herons lift and glide away, legs trailing,
their calls on the wind.

Ghost Dogs

Two hundred pounds apiece,
with strong bodies, great black heads,
and sad, sagging faces, they were my companions
through the long years of childhood.
Mastiffs. Herds of them—
studs, a handful of bitches, scores of puppies.
Bored, in dusty clumps, they guarded the driveway,
pulling themselves up
onto oversized padded feet
to trail my horse through the hills,
then—with surprising speed—racing
up deer trails in futile pursuit
of coyotes or bobcats.

My friends risked stitches in their thighs
by knocking on the door,
and when the proud cars of boyfriends pulled up—
a gleaming '68 Camaro, a convertible Bel Aire—
the pack ambushed them,
ferocious muzzles breathing steam,
drooling on the windows.

Now, all these years after leaving home,
I miss the dogs,
how formidable they were,
negotiating between me
and the world. I have
no silent creature at my side
to touch on her wrinkled brow,
no coiled animal to summon,
in love and ready to die.

Gone Sister

She never fell from her frantic mare
as it reared and twisted in the mustard fields.
And when she flipped out on acid, she didn't
plummet off a cliff at the end of Swift Street.

How could I help but admire her?
Nothing destroyed her—
not our father's fists knocking her out,
not our mother dressing her up
in lime-green jeans and torpedo bras,
sending her downtown to find the next
fatherless boy to serve as ranch-hand,
rake hay and move pipe
as Mother reached beneath his shirt.

Even if she was cast out at seventeen,
without family, she's still alive, sixty-six
in a jet-black wig and Grace Slick bangs—
the same as the day she threw
milk in our mother's face,
screamed up the driveway, left for good—
eyes inked with liquid liner,
lashes blackened, mouth slicked with gloss,
and open as if calling out.

White Hawk

Every day, the mourning doves
cooed their question—*Where? Where?*
but today, silence.

I filled the feeders
just after dawn, saw the patch
of fluffy down

on the grass below.
One wing feather with a black dot
told me who died.

Probably a hawk—
my favorite one,
the leucistic one—

plunged from the sky,
snatched up the dove,
then settled on the pine,

stood, gripping the blood-
pink neck, and shrieked
a call echoing

down the long valley.
That piebald raptor—
the one I've watched

for years, proud that she
chose to live above my field.
As if she were mine,

a totem, emblem of grace,
one who lifts me
from my thoughts,

stuns me on mornings
when I wake, dull, frightened
by my own emptiness,

how sharp and thin
the edges I balance on.
I hear her

shrill and alone,
drifting on the warm thermals
like the outstretched palm of a ghost.

Leaving the Burn Ward

It's strenuous to be vertical, to be outside
again in the glare of the parking lot reaching
for my mother's elbow.

The seats of the Lincoln Continental
are warm from the sun,
but I forget how to climb in,

so she bends my body to fit,
and I touch the blue leather,
aware that it's skin.

My tightly-wrapped forearms stretch on the rests,
while my legs, bound in pressure
garments reach across the carpeted floor.

Highway 17 terrifies me, twisting
through the coastal range,
the maples molting their yellow leaves.

Above the road, nets of heavy chain
constrain the crumbling cliffs, and as I pass,
the trees lean over and tremble.

The words I speak are nearly lost
in the hum of the V8:
Slow down, I say. *Turn off the radio.*

My mother complies, silent.
What can you say to a person
shocked by being alive?

Eighteen

Her mother, with whatever she used
against her children's shining faces—
flat of the palm, butter knives,
thin branches pruned from apple trees.
Her father watching, grim and satisfied—
they can't catch her.

She lives by the ocean now,
strips naked at midnight, slips out
the backdoor, runs to the edge
of the tide, her legs perfect
machines carrying her along the waves
all the way down the beach—
then a barefoot loop through the
silent neighborhood. Tar paper roofs,
like eyebrows, glower and bear down.

She can only be glimpsed
like a deer in a thicket, seen
for an instant, never found.

Chestnut Mare

I have no reason to walk
to the pasture anymore,
to stand at the gate,
calling her name,

to see her head swing up,
hear her nicker from wide nostrils
as she gallops toward me,
her thoroughbred muscles, precise
and angular, with a machine's strength,
churning beneath her glowing coat,

to grab a handful of mane,
swing onto her back, lie face up,
my legs dangling along her ribs,
while she drifts
with her own lazy purpose

out the gate,
eating clover and yellow vetch,
milk thistle and barley,
down to the full-flowing river,
my body becoming

the sound of her big teeth cutting grass,
her fur, musk like dusty alfalfa.

My life, her steady gait taking me
on some unknowable path.

III

Gorge

I was always hungry,
no, I wanted to be fed.
No, not that.
I wanted to be filled
once and for all, a man
filling me, a huge man,
stuffed completely by a man.
They couldn't, of course,
no one could,
they smelled something
on my breath, my need,
my arrogance.
Not arrogance,
derangement, thinking myself
supreme. Invulnerable. Royalty
to their temporary lust.
They knelt before me
before they took me
and left. I couldn't stop myself—
Four dozen brown-butter kringlers
from the Swedish Bakery,
half a cherry pie
from The Marketime Grocery,
where it smelled like sausages,
and I bounced checks.
I'd drive to an overlook
in Ballard, eat every bit
with a quart of milk.
I felt full, no, not full,
like I might die
if I hit my stomach
against the steering wheel.
Looking out on the blue

of the Sound, I saw Mount Olympus,
with its mantle of ice—like a god
I couldn't talk to.
Sitting in my car, I watched an old man
walking in a southwester, his nylon parka
covering him completely,
a small black Scottie dog
on a leash. I was jealous of them,
the way they aimlessly
took their way through
the lawn and wet rhododendron.
Couldn't stand to look at them.
Climbed in the backseat.
Pushed a cottony tampon down my craw,
held it with a string.
Careful. No fingernail
to make my throat bleed.
I felt beautiful
when my stomach decanted,
concave under my fingertips.
No, I didn't. I felt
like a lizard. When I breathed,
I smelled little pearls of vomit.
I felt hungry. No, I wanted to be fed,
no, I wanted a man. That's the way
I wanted it.

Alaska

In the mist above Unalaska, the last harbor
of the Aleutian ferry line, we hiked a tight path
carved in the side of a rocky escarpment, pocked
with dug-in bunkers where they'd shot down
kamikazes in World War II.

I was there with a man I didn't love anymore.
He'd hit my son, called my daughter a bitch.
I watched him walk in front of me on his thin ankles,
imagined my palms shoving his shoulder blades,
gravity destroying him on rocks
I barely saw below.

How easy it would be—
no dividing assets, no serving papers,
no $8,000 retainer to a chain-smoking lawyer.

But I knew I could never keep it quiet.
I love talking too much, letting myself out
into air and light
like a horse bucking from its stall.

That midnight, the light finally faded,
we staked a tent on an empty beach.
I pulled driftwood into a pile, dry and ready
for the touch of a match. The flames
shot up twenty feet, black smoke,
toxic as a venting volcano.

The dead trees were saturated with crude,
spilled decades before, a thousand miles away,
in some catastrophic wreck.

Disappearing

The way money does, or love, the dog
with her worn-out bone. How solid
and warm she felt as she begged
forgiveness with her red eyes,
parrot feathers stuck to her lips.
You don't want to admit this:
you trusted the world. In everything
making more of itself. Fairy rings.
Ringworm. Millions of wings.
The one mustard reseeding the meadow gold.
You learned how the universe expands
forever at greater and greater speeds,
felt lit by the neon gas of stars.

But you knew. Even a child knows:
The idea of endless inflation makes no sense.
You must concede to collapse, exposure
of a pale stratum—the earth's
green skin blasted to clay.
But still, don't you want to believe
you will never disappear? And by you
I mean all of us and everything we've made—
statues with broken arms and veiny feet,
oracles pointing their fingers on frescoed ceilings,
Pavarotti's tenor lifting from the chasm of common despair.

Look, you say, our world is as strong
as a beetle pushing a thousand times
its weight in dung. Isn't it better
to see the future as fierce joy?
Feel the wonder of knowing our gods

take guidance from other gods
who chose us. Us! Because we could
write their names in cuneiform,
shoot their images in sharp rockets
back to their own hearts.

French Kiss

*The study . . . reconstructs the first microbiomes from an
extinct hominin species, and hints at intimacy—perhaps
kisses—between humans and Neanderthals.*
  —Ewen Callaway in Nature, 08 March 2017

Of course, I learned it from him,
that husky meat-eater downstream,
with his sprung chest and hairy thighs.
Beautiful brute on the other side
of the river, whom I watched in secret
on hot Pleistocene days
as he cared for the elderly,
soothed the deformed and wounded,
protected infants from our packs of wild dogs.

My heart found its raw beginning
the day I saw him toss wildflowers on a grave,
his feet solid on the young earth
as he gripped bluebonnets and dandelions,
a few bruised roses in his beefy fists.

Who cares if he never learned
the finer points of moss eating
or sometimes went cannibal.
Wasn't he kinder? Gentler
than our gangs of village boys
who returned, riled from the hunt,
the bloody thighs of megafauna
humped home on their slimy backs.

So I ventured out one night and found him
at the edge of a bonfire's light, grabbed
the smooth pelt glossing his barrel back,
pulled him to my breasts and tongued him.

I kissed that man from Neander Valley
long and slow, delighted in the clout of his jaw,
the muscled capture of his lips, his fragrant
saliva, thick like some forgotten vintage.

Don't tell me I'm fetishizing the Other.
I'm through with Homo Sapien men.
Though my terrible uncles slaughtered
every one of his tribe,
I'll carry him in my mouth forever.

Pinwheel the Cockatiel

before she died, spoke fluent English
like a beauty contestant babbling
about world peace, causing my then-husband
to fall in love as she sat on his hand,
nibbled his ear, preened him,
never mistaking his fingers for Brazil nuts.

I found the cockatiel on the floor of the cage
her beak around a thin bar as if trying
to pull herself from the weeds that sprouted
in rotted seed he'd thrown into the guano.

It was no use
asking him to put the bird food
in its yellow cup, to change
the newspaper and tainted water.
How many times had she escaped?
How many times had he charmed her
back into her hutch, by waiting
all night beneath the pine tree as she sang
my name from the far branches.

Man Flies Solo in a Stolen Plane

from a New York Times article, August 11, 2018

While he was aloft, the man spoke
of the beauty he saw.
The Olympics, Mount Rainier,
The Cascades—how silent
they were, aloof,
still full of winter snow.
He worried aloud about jail time,
his rapidly fading gas tank,
chatted with air traffic controllers
about his hopes for a *moment of serenity*
but, instead, he lamented,
the sights *went by so fast.*
He'd wanted to barrel roll,
wondered if the plane could backflip.
I got a lot of people who care about me,
and it's gonna disappoint them to hear I did this... Just
a broken guy, I guess.
Got a few screws loose.
Never really knew it until now.
Southwest of the airport, he found an empty island,
crashed there and died.

Who said that life is a plummet
from a church's roof to its graveyard?
The whole time craving a tremor of peace,
pride in one perfect trick, taking in
the details as they fly by, faster
and faster in the fall—blur of billboards
with Bible verses from John, big ships
passing under the belly of sky, glimpses
of river birches turning their coins
in the cold wind.

Ode to the Dog

It's been millennia.
This love of stick and chase.
Pack love. Love of wild meat
Run down and flame blackened.
Warmth of fire,
The way we lay together
At the line between flickering heat and fear,
Your dirty fur close
Against our naked skin.

Forty thousand years, they say,
Since you came to our aid,
Wiping out the Neanderthal,
Thinning their game,
Grafting four-legged speed
To the guile of our strange brains.
Forty thousand years side-by-side
Since you left your wild
Brother wolf for us.

We see that sometimes
When you forget who you are—
Snap at a kitten or clamp your teeth
Around the jeaned thigh of a stranger.
Or we notice in your fulsome eyes
What you've lost
When you slink into shame,
Accept choke chains and neglect.

And don't we also pay a price?
Our human lifespans so much longer—
We must watch the same old friend,
Again and again, die a different death.

Ex

I glimpsed him leaving Trader Joe's,
loading his disposable brown bag of stuff
into his wax-buffed Jag. My ex—
his face dehydrated now,
in the way of those old-timey applehead dolls.
This was the guy
to whom I cried as we did it—*Take me*
any way you want me. So loud an exaltation
that it carried for acres—
into the neighborhood chapel,
where it shivered the sainted windows.
All the way into abandoned apartments,
awakening tweakers with their smoky pipes.
Into the fragrance of espresso bars
serving absinthe and squirts of whiskey syrup,
the pierced baristas pausing
as they plunged the steamer rod
into the teased-up milk.
That's how it is when you're a woman
in your prime. You vocalize.
Especially after all the years I spent
with a man who walked out
the bedroom door while I waited
in bra and panties, posing to show
the curve of my waist, the peach
lace of my Victoria's Secret—
my jars of vulva balm going rancid
on the bedside table.

After my great plague of nothing, the first
to uncork the fine champagne
of my lust. There he was again,

his blotched arms heaving
Friskies cat food
onto the smooth leather of his backseat.

College Field Study

Once I led a blind man down a river toward a place called Paradise.
We were in the western Sierras, and I wanted him—
after studying meadows full of purple shooting stars—
to play naked with me in a swimming hole,
a place where students dove from twenty-foot peaks
into pools of pebbled quartz, electric cold, where we slid
down slabs into ice-melt streams.

I loved his voice, like a tearless sob, how he spoke of nothingness—
not even lightning bug flashes on the underside of his lids.
I loved to hear how strippers availed their bodies to him to be brailled,
how his wife was glad he couldn't see her, only touch her,
how possessive she was, not wanting him there, eight thousand feet up.

I mapped a path, led him to the water, turned him downstream,
described each step, while he used my eyes to make his way
beside me. He asked to sit for a while on a rock and listen
to a black-headed grosbeak and the sound of the creek.
What do you see? he asked me. Light-yellow azaleas. *They smell like roses.*

Then we carried on, his feet probing the ground, palm on my shoulder.
I told him to hop off a small edge on the riverbank. Just a little drop.
He didn't take my hand. Smiling, he looked into his emptiness
and leapt. Maybe he thought it was five inches when it was more like a foot.
Afterwards, he sat, twisted, holding his ankle. *Go,* he said. *Go on without me.*

I can't remember how he returned to camp.

The next day, I jumped boulder to boulder
and headed back to Paradise alone
where the speckled trout waited mute under rocky ledges
flickering away when I invaded their world.

Membership

It's weird to be a member of an invasive species,
accumulating sky miles and slurping Starbucks.
Weird to be within my skin, yet part
of a horde, colony, swarm in search
of sugar, creating commerce as it goes.
My activewear unspools its filaments,
fills the mouths of salmon, remains
in their guts like undigested worms.
I dream of generations pouring out
of my womb—shining insects,
their hungry mandibles eating
from a trough of strange corn.
Now, the night is bereft of music
I've almost forgotten—
hosts of frogs belching love,
slip of salamander
into the cold grip of stream.
The color of the sky today
like something scraped from
the walls of a collapsed hive—
golden elixir acquired
with the last coin sewn into my coat.

IV

Everything That's Old

Jets are the new motorhomes
chemtrails are the new clouds
the unknown dead on an island
are the calm before a storm
robots are the new immigrants
Roundup is the new hoe
Colbert is the new Cronkite
smoke is the new sky
drought is the new summer
cars are heart disease
dust is lawn
downtown is the new homeless
Amazon, the new mall
retired is the new nomad
needles are the new rusty nail
plastic, the new lead
viral, the new headline
posting, the new protest
the horizon of the western ocean
is the new ghost of Godzilla
the Cold War is the new Cold War
fire heading down a suburban street
is wind
anxiety is the new air
the Earth's crust is the weak eggshell
of a songbird.

Replacements

...*We live by symbolic*
substitution.
                    —Frank Bidart

Even if it isn't true, I like to believe
my body replaces itself every seven years,
my sloughed-off flakes of skin
filling the house with fragments
of my younger self.

I like to feel how my kidneys, nestled
in their watery caves, labor to rebuild
while I vacuum and straighten, throw away
books about tantric sex, with their
soft drawings of young women
arching their backs and biting their lips. All the men,
well-built, attentive like hypnotized jewelers.

And the world, too, seems so different—
no more jays on phone lines
haranguing over the compost heap.
Instead, a coarse string of crows complains.
And in the field, a bull fattens,
shaking his head at flies
in the exact place where my beautiful horse
once grazed—the one I bought
after my lover left me for a better woman.

Again and again, the leaving.
Look at my father, as he slowly died,
his lips thinned and slid higher up his teeth.
The shape of his face became oblong,
and his hands fisted into paralyzed fury
as his basal brain meat failed him.

At the time, I felt nothing but the crumbling
of some distant bulwark. But seven years later,
I seem to hear my father's phlegmy growl. I see him again
in the tufted muzzle of the wire-haired bitch
I found at the pound—the same gray mane
and bulldog face—leashed, mostly under control.

Apple Orchard

—*for Danusha Laméris*

For it was hot, the air thick
with vermin smell,
and the field, an abattoir
whose perimeter I walked
with a poet and a young dog
we'd released from a coop
where the neighbor kept her
day after day in guano and dirt.

For on the first loop, we saw
a small pile, an awful shade of rust—
feathers, beak, and thin ribs
broken into the soil.
And the dog, with joy, ran
to roll her wire hair in it.
All endings moldered there,
alone as god in the dust,
and we both sought
to name it—
turken, silkie, Rhode Island red.
We smelled its linger, flat
and crotchy, beckoning flesh flies.

For on the second turn, we spied
a green-glowing tail feather
and clumps of down.
We walked the rim of a predator's plate.
Coyote, I said, but she said, *Mountain lion.*
She'd seen its eyes
by the bridge at midnight, heard its
pitched scream like a terrified woman.

For on the third lap, we saw
a chewed tibia
with cured strips of fascia
holding to the slender bone,
at its tip, a fawn's cloven hoof,
shell-black with a blue sheen.

The crickets keened heat.
Ticks dropped from the trees,
we brushed them off the bare skin
of each other's shoulders,
picked them from the pup's soft belly.

The deer foot is yours, she said.
And I carried it, waiting
for it to speak as the dog leapt—
for all things mention themselves,
even if they've been silenced
or have no mouths.

Looking

We live our lives in one place
and look in every moment into another.
— Jane Hirshfield

I used to beg my parents to drive through suburbs,
so I could stare at tract homes, the bland windows
and porticos full of tipped-over trikes. I liked
to parse the three or four different house models,
study the flourishes—garden statues of seven dwarves,
shrubs like poodles, wagon wheels
resting on white-quartz lawns.
It made me sick how much I wanted it—
a mom with fixed-up hair,
a dad in an apron holding a Hamm's,
flipping spare ribs. A cul-de-sac
full of boys shooting hoops, little girls
holding hands because they couldn't bear
to unbraid their shared delight.
Different from the dirt farm
where I felt lucky to escape for one day
the slash of a horsewhip, where
I was told to carry my plate to the floor,
eat my dinner next to five sad mastiffs,
each of us gulping a slab of freshly butchered bull heart.
I must have been crazy to return to that ranch,
raise my twins there, close
to the smell of mountain lilac and chicken shit.
The woman who looked itchy as she beat me
became a doting grandmother who fed them
homemade cheese on Red Delicious, bought them
pink and blue Oshkosh from catalogues,
walked them through pastures to touch
the nose of a newborn Jersey.
And now, more than half-a-century past, my mother
still stares out her window at the pigsty, curdles

her milk, and stirs the whey with a wooden spoon.
It's hard to believe I'm here too, slouched
in the spruced-up barn near dying oaks and a cow field,
drinking pots of bitter tea and looking at families
on Facebook holding up goblets of yellowy wine
or standing on Half Dome, arms lifted like gods.

I stay so she can call me when she falls
or needs to talk about the hawk that drops down
and rips the neck of her pampered bantam,
her pain, almost too much to bear.

Thanksgiving

I don't know what to think
about my face anymore.
I think *giblets*. No that's not it:
Wattles. Wattle's the word.
The word for what dangles
from a bird. A bird who seemed prideful
of those blood-engorged genitalia-
like clots hanging from
his beaky chin. A horny turkey
spotting me, his target—
a small farm girl
in a dress, lacy like feathers.
He ran like a jet
taking off on a runway,
wattles shaking like a flag
in a hot wind. Flew like victory,
like hunger. Onto my back, held
my neck with his sharp yellow beak
as I lay there trapped
under his sex.

Now, I have trembly bags
under my face. I've turned
the crone corner, shaken hands
with the new old me. I'd like
to finish up here, and
say why that's OK.
Because I've seen worse,
and I've seen better. Been around.

Sixty years ago, a huge turkey
tried to rape me. My sister slammed him
with a shovel, he sailed over the garden fence
his gobble-call fading into the faraway, before
he landed delicious on my plate.

Older Sister

I'd watch her insert her falsies,
draw the arch line of an eyebrow, check
the tightness of her ass with a hand mirror.
Then grab her fringed purse and drive
downtown to find some feral boy
who'd hitchhiked to California
all the way from Tennessee.

I believed in her beauty, the way
she wielded her mascara wand
like a lance. Walked like a warrior
into womanhood.

But I knew I couldn't do it—tried to stop
it from happening, refused
to bathe, snacked day and night
on crisp biscuits, sucked my thumb.
Howled with the dogs.

Now I've unblocked her on Facebook
to see what she's up to, if her face
has lined like mine, how her neck
and chest are weathering.

In the throes of new romance, she's pretty hot,
sporting a wig to the waist and spaghetti-strap tee.
In one profile pic, a man cradles her
like he owns her. She's a lean cat
in a close-fit leopard-print pajama.
She lengthens her neck, purses her lips,
shows her dimples to the camera.

Every few minutes, I click back to peek again—
her proud smile, her fingers in the victory V.
I'm an old apostate watching a lost ritual.
I can't stop staring at her lit room from the outside.

Stubble

I shave my whiskers.
It's not a shame, not frightening.
In fact, I found it funny, years ago,
when my then-husband walked in—
my face lathered, straight blade in hand—
and he said, *Goddamnit.*
Do you have to do that in front of me?

That was maybe a year before he left,
with little fight or fanfare. Just gave up.

But there's none of that for me,
not while I beach my body
each morning into the dense gravity of living,
look in the mirror at my pale fallen face,
framed by a white mist of hair
and spot the unstoppable,
insistent grey and glistening
stubbles—more every year.

What I fear is what might happen
if I fell into a coma, without my own hand
to slide the clean blade over the bristles,
chin hair stringy like a vine
crawling over a dead house.

But for now I don't bother
to pluck. I prefer to mow, not weed.
Although, they say plucking
would root the things out—
once and for all—
like miniscule mandrakes torn
from oily pits in my flesh.

Dogs

Curled in hot dust, muzzles tucked under tails,
skin flicking flies, we see them lie close
at the feet of Vietnam vets who stand
in meridians with bent cardboard signs.

The demands of the anxious,
the accusations hurled at the unblinking sky—
dogs don't care—warm-eyed, waiting,
they gaze at the ones who keep them.

Maybe there was a time we loved like that,
before monuments and wheat, wheels, and fire,
before we wanted a separate power held
in our pink-skinned palms.

When we walked on padded paws in packs, tracking
meat to feed on side by side, sat together
through solstice nights, howling at the bad moon.

Romance and Physics

His head haloed by the dark smell leading to my womb,
his face glazed with craving, his ordinary
shoulders and soft freckled paunch, transformed,
gilded with sweat and musk—
to be wanted like that
was rotgut ethanol, and I was parched for the burn,
its quick trip to my head, the way
the world glistered, suddenly lit and particulate.

How I loved hearing his theories
of lasers and micron-sized beads, how
the fabric of spacetime curved.
To watch him squint over equations,
long straight lines of them, written with fine-tip pens
on paper ripped from Mead writing tablets,
fallen in piles like dead leaves
around his busted sofa. Every new piece,
a clean slate graphed with hope for an elegant solution.
It's you and me, Baby, he'd say,
fists gripped as he swaggered like a gunslinger.
When I asked him to take his boots
off the couch, he yelled, *Bitch,*
you're hysterical.
It made me want him more,

feeling sure he was some kind of kin—
born on the same cruel
day in April as my sister,
dark-haired like my mother, trip-wired for fistfights,
all the elements of my distemper.

How powerful I thought I was, believing
that with my itch and my need
I could bend back time to the moment
I broke free of my mother's body,
to be spawned anew into a parallel world
where I could live clean,
untouched and redeemed.

V

Yellow

It's February, and the acacia
is blooming. Not wet,
though winter's well along,
and the flowers by now
should be cold and sodden.
No matter. The air is helpless,
punch-drunk with pollen.
I know what's next—
rooty mustard. Fields of it
mixed with the weightless
mouths of sour grass
showing their throats
as they shift on listless stems.
Yellow's the first color of spring.
Hope yellow. Sick yellow.
Kitchen yellow. Pollen-petaled heart
of the columbine yellow, she-lost-
her-mind-and-ran-away-with-the-
pearl-handled-kitchen-knives yellow.
Head home to California
on the Gray Rabbit bus line,
from Seattle to San Francisco,
seats stripped-out, hippies
on dirty mattresses,
spooning and massaging
above the hum of the drivetrain.
Stop at Crescent City, stand
on a ridge, above a full-bloom meadow.
All that yellow
feeding my brain after nothing
but pine and pewter-grey.
I'm home. Thirty years now,

the rain behind me,
but I'm calling for it
down from the north
to scrub the thick air,
dampen the dried loam.
I'm too old to climb
the silver-skinned acacias,
botched with notches of crumbly black,
to sit thirty feet up
and scratch the bark's thin skin,
smell the whiskey-wood stink,
see the hard green beneath,
smooth as muscle on an athlete's arms.
To bower myself, safe
between limb and trunk
like I did when I was six,
thinking nothing could touch me.
Not strange weather,
not whatever way the world ends.

Burn Survivor Auguries

Once you smelled smoke,
        turned around. Your
        chenille bathrobe flared up, loud,
        and began to consume you.

Now, whatever you see shimmering on the horizon, or hear
        buzzing in the fire of electric wires
        throbs a thin message in your ears.

Nothing portends only itself. If swallows cease
        stitching the sky,
        what else might happen?

Look up, there are fumes threading needles of jets—
        sunset staining the streaks garnet
        like bags of blood
        ready for transfusion,

donated to the leaking well of your body
        by strangers who offered up
        the pale undersides of their arms,
        so something cold could enter them,
        so they could enter you.

What became smoke—tips of fingers, the nail bed,
        the sole of your right foot,
        all the skin from neck to knee—

you might be breathing it right now. No wonder
        you see yourself everywhere.

Band-tailed Pigeon

I stand in the searing heat
in my beat-up robe,
ready to fill the depleted feeders,
with bags of mealworm, millet,
black-oil seeds, and suet—

when I see it—big as a boot,
wings beating like a raptor's
as it drops into my dried-out garden,
scattering chickadees and bushtits,
sending up a pulse of quail.

White crescent on her hind-neck
a block of pink-checkered shine,
she turns her nape to the sun, shows
her dove-gray chest, palest rose
like dusty silk.

So like a passenger pigeon,
for a minute I think Miracle!
A Lazarus bird has returned.

Sixty years living here, I've never
seen this city-hater hazard flight
out of the buckeye poison and tick trees
where they gather and thrum,

weave sticks nesting single eggs,
yolks scavenged by jays,
hatchlings, murdered and switched
with changeling cowbirds.

Look what it's come to—
kids grown, my father dead,
a mother too old to hate,
two husbands gone, memories
of a lover slivered in my gut
like shards I can't work out.

Waiting for another clumsy visitor
from a place I thought was empty—
cousin to a glowing steel-grey ghost.
So fearful and so hungry.

At Sixty-Two

Looking at my X-ray, the doctor
says my hips resemble
those of an eighty-year-old woman.

Weeks later, when I huff into a tube
to blow out virtual birthday candles,
my allergist mentions
with what seems smug satisfaction
that my lungs whistle
like an eighty-year-old woman's.

O hypothetical eighty-year-old woman—
you skeletal model
walking the hospital runway
in this year's open-assed robe
of blue-dotted cotton—
how do you like being the *It Girl of Mortality,*

archetype of *You are nearly nothing?*

I want a physician who lists my body's features
like a used-car pitch—
> *here's a real beaut, light-pink '62*
> *Plymouth Valiant with a push-button*
> *transmission, perky butt fins,*
> *cat-print leather interior,*
> *spurs hanging from the mirror,*
> *and tires with some tread—*

and its driver, an aging prima ballerina,
rose-red hair and rhinestone glasses,
> out for a spin
> on a racetrack,

falling behind while fans applaud
for old-time's sake,
        looping and looping
before she veers off through a cow field.

Tanny and Yankee

As a child, my bedsheets were gritty
with fleas. The dog sighed,
warm and wire-haired by my legs.
I popped in my thumb and sucked, pretended
my hands were ducks.
When my needy mouth let go, they flew—
little living glove puppets with smiling beaks.

They landed in my hair, and my
head became a factory, turning
my red tresses to brass wire.
Some threads were gold.
Find the beautiful strands! said Yankee
to the lazy left-hand Tanny.

All those summer afternoons, alone
with my books, flies hitting the hot window, I sucked.
At sixteen, still, when my crush cheated, when my
best friend moved away, it soothed me
to slip in dear Yankee and nurse.

In my twenties, on the long commute home,
I leaned on the steering wheel, sucking
like a sleepy toddler until
my thumb wrinkled, pale and clean.
At thirty-four, I gave it up—my fattest digit no longer
rested on my tongue.

O Yankee, my right-hand man, the boss
who slept in my mouth. I miss him!
Even though he's here, writing
his memoir with a fine-tip pen.
He remembers me with nostalgia,
the child he raised.

Birdman

Every morning, my Amazon parrot greets me
as he has since the day I bought him
for ten bucks on a dusty road
with his downcast rage and broken wing.

Hello Birdman, I say, and from his iron cage
he chirps like a telephone, lowers his yellow head,
so I can scratch the down
beneath his pin feathers, lift him
to my lips for a clucky kiss.

For over four decades, he's hated
first my boyfriends, then my husbands, three dogs, and a cat.
On the October morning when I carried my swaddled
twins into the sunroom and set them in the bassinet,
he stared with one yellow eye, tilted his head,
raked the air with his screams. Oh, he's full of loathing,
my little green man.

How could he have known— as he flew
above the *milpas* in Hermosillo, before some kid
shot off his wing—that for the rest of his life,
he would live with a giant companion
looming over him with heavy
bones and fleshy claws.

And how could I have known my prince
would fill a space in the chaos
three inches wide and eight inches long, that he would
kiss me at dawn with his Bakelite beak and
dry tongue—wear a plumed suit the color of lawn.

Another Happiness

Publish your best work, find a decent job.
Eat some sizzling octopus, the many
kissing tentacles meaty on your tongue.
Success, you think, *Joy!* For a while anyway,
then it's another mess in the papers, the endless
scroll of rapists and dead turtles, another
photo of a world leader with his corn-baked face.

So you go on a car trip north to find
some good rain. You get to Seattle,
and the lawns are scab-brown,
your old home on the lake—a lime-green high rise.
Always looking for something.
Answer keys. Antidepressants.
More friends, another dog, another slim poetry book
where the poet keeps pushing and pushing,
line after line of exquisite description, one astonished
metaphor after another, escalating into an ecstatic revelation.

You can't write like that.
You don't read enough Virgil and Milton, don't start
your day writing lines of iambic pentameter.
Detroit, Detroit, Detroit, Detroit, Detroit.
And you can't meditate like some of the big names do.
When you sit, it feels like termites streaming in and out
of your arteries. On the screen of your inner vision,
all your arrogance, ecstasy, and gloom.
Your crappy conversations with the bitches in Zumba Gold
telling you to irrigate your nostrils, get therapy,
put a prong collar on your mutt.

But admit it—sometimes in fall, you look up and see
an arrowhead of duck flight, lonesome and luxurious.
If only you could understand
how fungus flowers from the mind of the land,
how fractal arms of trees shard the sky.
If only you could exalt
in ash falling, the West on fire,
it would be like you'd just arrived on earth.

Silbar

means whistle. A Spanish word
that sounds like silver
in the air, a little bird's song
Oh My Dear. Oh My Dear.
Every year, the first time I hear
that smooth *silbato,*
it's the first day of fall, a sparrow
with a small stripe lining its eye,
passing through
with the dying days
when the golden apple's skin
feels softer than in summer,
a little more honey.
Oh My Dear. Little girl,
this is how it begins—
school, getting up early, not knowing
what you're in for,
what your friends will do to you,
what you'll do to them,
what being one year older
will mean in the world
of a girl. What to fear
and what to hope for.

Walk into the side of a mountain—
some cave of limestone and chert.
As the sparrow sings,
light a fire. It's cold outside.
Let flames flick the ceiling
with ghosts of wild gazelles,
grab some coal, some ochre
the color of crusty blood
and a rabbit's thigh bones to trace them—

stickmen running with laughing legs,
spears carried high above their heads.
See who walks out
alive in spring.

Safety

No bone snapped clean,
no bare-chested bully,
no bell calling you in.
No blaring heat. Safe,
your blood warm, abandoned
dog at your feet.
A husband who loves you
like a bird's nest of careful eggs.
You can stand, blank, letting light
beam over the battered face
of everything, the barbed
nettles, tarred leaves
of the bay tree, the pitter
of river birches
raining their catkins.
You can feel how broken you are.
You can't be happy
in all this quiet. It frightens you,
knowing salvation
is a point of light
the eye follows downstream.
Not God, not the angry men
you fell in with, not the mother
who silenced you
with backhands and bruises,
not the bile-green bitterness
you learned to carry
close like your own beloved.
How can you forget
the look of the sky
as they beat you?
Telling you nothing
of the beauty in your flesh.

You've heard it takes one person
loving a child
for a child to survive,
and you say, *Even if it's just a dog.*
It might be enough—
this wind you listen to, the thin limbs.
Whatever it was
that was given you
that you don't know you have.

Low Tide

A dog finds a piece of kelp
among the starfish,

a brown hollow weed
twenty feet long.
At one end, bulky

as a light bulb,
thin like twine at the tip.
She drags it over the sand

running from her owner,
who calls and calls,
uselessly, it seems.

Such a happy dog,
frenzied by her precious prize
of stinky tube,

full of soft gelatinous sea,
too large for the car,
impossible to take home—

this segment of a vast world
between her sharp teeth.

All the Hungry Falcons

Appetite makes them keen
when they scan the tunneled field
for shivers in the dead grass.
Their vision sharpens, pupils dilate.
From a mile away, they see
their feed, and they take it.
All my life, I've stowed my stories
like a box of banned books
under the bed. Each one, unforgiven,
an arc of trouble and want.
They quicken my hunger
for what I'll never have
or never have again—
a mother mainly, certain men,
but a sister and brother too, a city
I walked in with hot paper cups,
my lips foamed with cappuccino
as it rained and rained.
Oh, the world feels tidal
when I get like this, when l can't stop
hunting for something intimate and filling.
I see it lift from the soil.
The sun, a muzzle flash,
turning the meadow bright, burning
off the haze. I soar in, see it magnified,
everything itself only more so.

Acknowledgments

Thank you to the following journals where poems from this collection, sometimes in different versions, first appeared.

Atlanta Review: "Chestnut Mare"

Canary: "Band-tailed Pigeon," "Musth," "Rivervale,"and "White Hawk"

Catamaran: "Another Happiness" and "Mare in the Road"

Crab Creek Review: "Disappearing"

Massachusetts Review: "Insides"

Nailed: "Looking"

New Letters: "Alaska," "Gorge," and "Romance and Physics"

New Ohio Review: "At Sixty-Two," "Liberal Father," and *"Silbar"*

Porter Gulch Review: "Afterlife" and "Dead Dog"

R.kv.ry: "Gone Sister"

Rattle: "Everything That's Old"

Red Wheelbarrow: "Birdman" and "Pinwheel the Cockatiel"

Spillway: "Leaving the Burn Ward"

SWWIM: "All the Hungry Falcons"

The SUN: "Ghost Dogs"

Typishly: "Ex"

Universal Table: "Scars"

What Rough Beast: "Dogs," "French Kissing, "Membership," "Ode to the Dogs," "Scavenged," and "Why Did I Call My Pig"

"Scars" was published in *Longer Than Expected: Adulthood After Life Threatening Childhood Illness* (Wising Up Press, 2017).

"Afterlife," "Everything That's Old," and "Ghost Dogs," were reprinted in *phren-Z Literary Magazine,* summer 2018.

"Birdman" was reprinted in *A Constellation of Kisses,* ed. Diane Lockward (Terrapin Books 2019).

"Everything That's Old" was reprinted in *Recovering Words, Sisyphus,* and *Tribach.*

"Leaving the Burn Ward," "Mare in the Road," "Safety," and "White Hawk" were reprinted in *phren-Z,* spring 2019.

"Why Did I Call My Pig" was reprinted in *Canary.*

"Alaska" was featured on *Verse Daily* on November 8, 2019.

"All the Hungry Falcons" was featured on *Women's Voices for Change,* November, 2019.

"Ex" was featured on *The Central Coast Poetry Show,* August 13, 2019.

My gratitude to Ken Symes of Western Washington University who, forty years ago, not only told me I could write, but also exhorted me to respect the gift. I've never forgotten you, I hope this book finds you. To Ellen Bass, who allowed that, although it was "cruel" to say it, I could be a writer if I tried. To my super fun friend and mentor, Danusha Laméris, who continually reminds me that to independently evaluate one's own work is the supreme skill. To my buddies in the Santa Cruz workshops: Julie Murphy, Kim Scheiblauer, JoAnn Birch, Julia Chiapella, Lisa Charnock, Donna Murray, Cynthia White, Nancy Miller Gomez, Erin Redfern, Pat Zyllius, Amanda Moore, Jory Post, Q of the Continuum, and all the rest. To Kwame Dawes, Joe Millar, Ellen Bass, and Dorianne Laux for helping me shape the poems that became

Ghost Dogs. Thank you also to my Pacific University platoon of fellow writers: Megan Walch, Ann Mairoff, Emily Tobias, Cynthia Neeley, Julia B. Levine, Emily Ransdell, Shari McDonald, Sarah Sexton, Nicole Barney, and Lisa Allen Ortiz for such badass support in the trenches. To the Queen Bees of The Hive Poetry Collective and all the guests who teach me every time—thanks for the honey. To my mother, father, and sister—you became my muses. To Jill, the wrangler. To all the ghost dogs who tried to protect me. And always, to my loves—Arthur, Darrian, and Michael.

About the Author

Dion O'Reilly has lived most of her life on a small farm in the Soquel Valley of California. She has studied with Ellen Bass and Danusha Laméris and received her MFA from Pacific University. For over thirty years, she worked as a school teacher, also leading private groups for her high school students. Her poetry and essays have appeared in *The Massachusetts Review, New Letters, Sugar House Review, Rattle, The Sun, Bellingham Review, New Ohio Review, Catamaran, SWWIM, Grist,* and other literary journals and anthologies. She is a member of The Hive Poetry Collective which produces podcasts highlighting poets from the Monterey Bay and around the world. She hosts classes for adults on her farm. *Ghost Dogs* is her debut full-length collection.

www.dionoreilly.wordpress.com

CPSIA information can be obtained
at www.ICGtesting.com
Printed in the USA
FSHW022035300120
66511FS